# - Acts of Kindness Tracker -

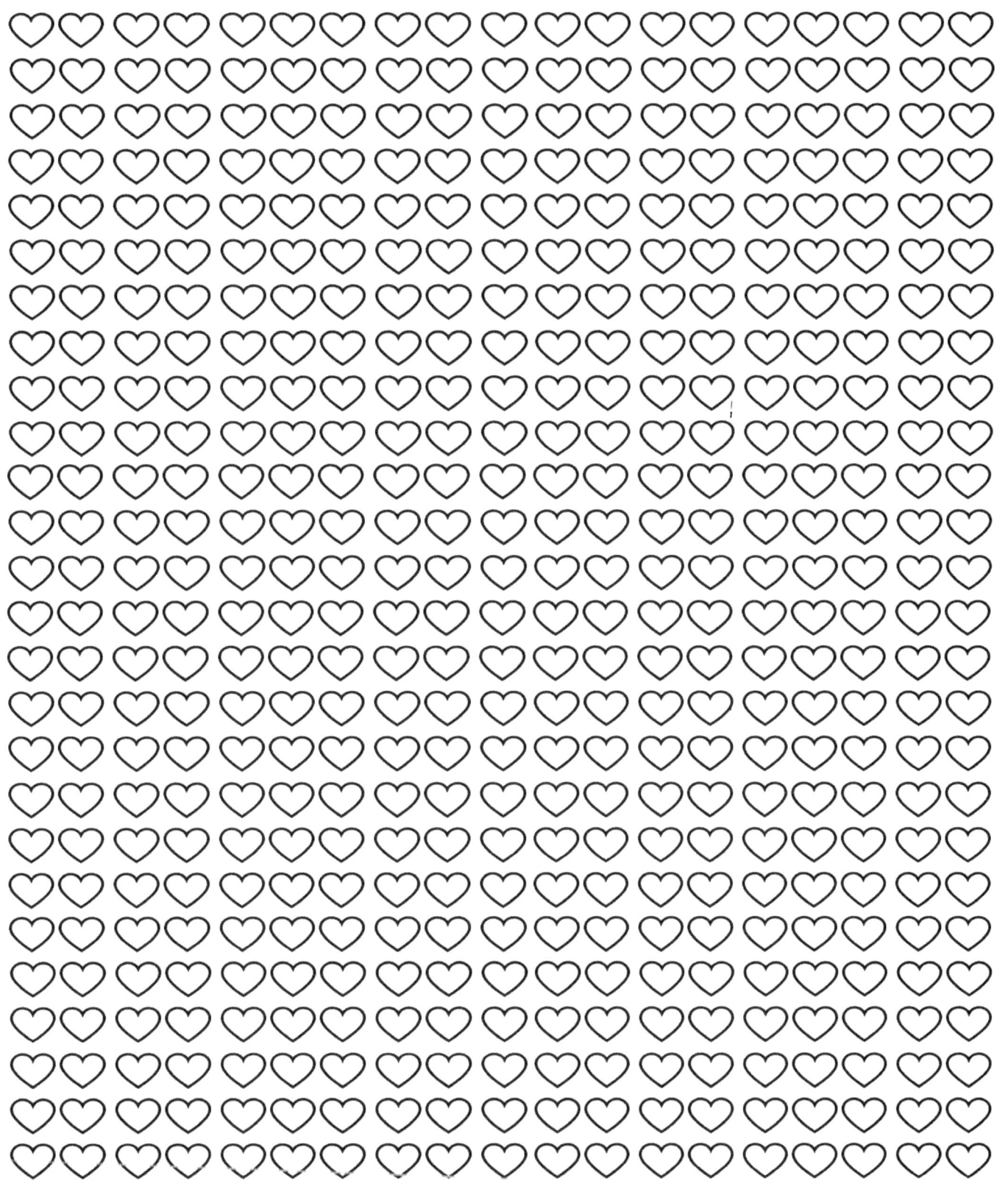

# - Acts of Kindness Tracker -

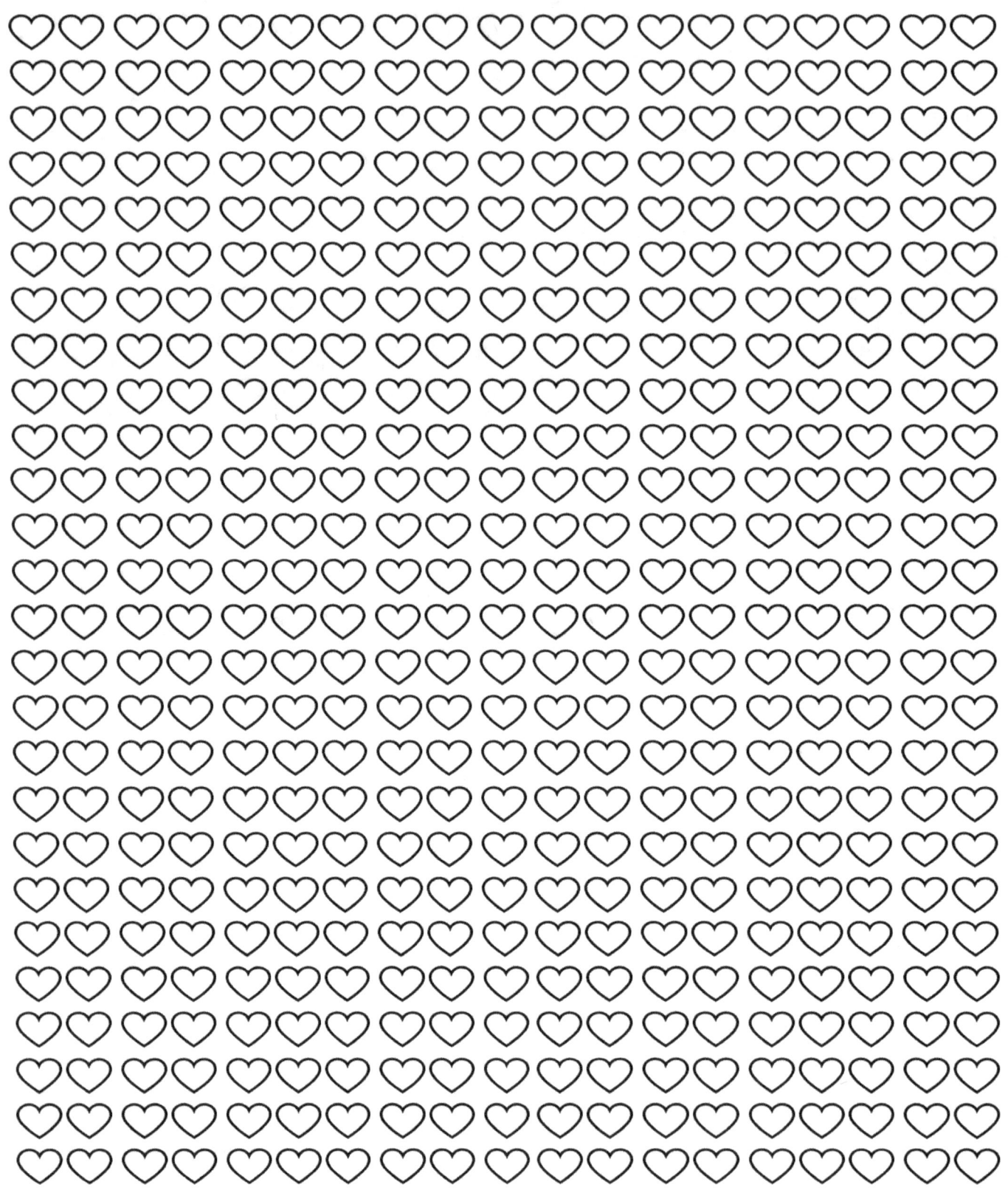

# - Acts of Kindness Tracker -

# Notes

# Notes

# Notes

www.ingramcontent.com/pod-product-compliance
Lightning Source LLC
LaVergne TN
LVHW060140080526
838202LV00049B/4038

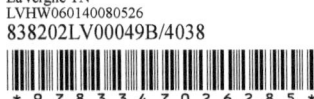